KENTUCKY WILDCATS

BY BRIAN HOWELL

Printed in the United States of America,
North Mankato, Minnesota
102011
012012

THIS BOOK CONTAINS AT LEAST 10% RECYCLED MATERIALS.

Editor: Chrös McDougall
Copy Editor: Bo Smolka
Design and production: Craig Hinton

Photo Credits: Orlin Wagner/AP Images, cover; AP Images, 1, 4, 7, 9, 15, 19, 42 (top right), 43 (top); Art Shay/Sports Illustrated/Getty Images, 10, 42 (top left); H.B. Littlell/AP Images, 17; Rich Clarkson/Sports Illustrated/Getty Images, 20, 25, 26, 42 (bottom); James Crisp/AP Images, 23; Tim Sharp/AP Images, 28; Dave Martin/AP Images, 31, 41, 43 (bottom right); Rich Clarkson/NCAA Photos/AP Images, 33; Charlie Neibergall/AP Images, 34; Eric Draper/AP Images, 37, 43 (bottom left); Mark Humphrey/AP Images, 39; Ed Reinke/AP Images, 44

Design elements: Matthew Brown/iStockphoto

Library of Congress Cataloging-in-Publication Data
Howell, Brian, 1974-
Kentucky Wildcats / by Brian Howell.
p. cm. -- (Inside college basketball)
Includes index.
ISBN 978-1-61783-284-0
1. University of Kentucky--Basketball--History--Juvenile literature. 2. Kentucky Wildcats (Basketball team)--History--Juvenile literature. I. Title.
GV885.43.U53H68 2012
796.323'630976947 B--dc23
2011039987

TABLE OF CONTENTS

Kentucky junior forward Johnny Cox averaged 14.9 points per game for Kentucky during the 1958 season.

1

IMPROBABLE CHAMPS

THE UNIVERSITY OF KENTUCKY MEN'S BASKETBALL TEAM HAS WON MORE GAMES THAN ANY OTHER TEAM IN COLLEGE BASKETBALL HISTORY. MANY OF THE WILDCATS' WINS CAME UNDER THE DIRECTION OF COACH ADOLPH RUPP.

Rupp won 876 games during his 41 seasons in charge. He coached some very talented teams along the way. Still, not even Rupp thought the 1958 Wildcats would win as much as they did. The Wildcats were ranked in the top 10 in the country most of the season. However, few thought they had championship material.

"We weren't expected to go anywhere with that team," Rupp said. "I didn't expect to. I think the boys were the only ones that thought they'd go anywhere and I don't think they were too sure about this thing. We didn't have a lot of support anywhere. This bunch of kids, they just kept winning."

Rupp called his starting group "The Fiddlin' Five." That was because they often did not play well early in games.

"They just fiddled around and fiddled around and finally, with about two or three minutes to play, they'd get busy and they'd win a ball game," Rupp said. "Just about killed me. I'll tell you, that was a bone-crushing season for me."

Looking back, perhaps the third game of that season should have been a clue that the Wildcats were in for a special season. It was on December 7, 1957. Playing at home in Lexington, Kentucky, the Wildcats fell behind Temple, 71–69, with one second to play in overtime. The Wildcats fans figured the game was pretty much over.

"The fans now begin to pour for the exits," radio announcer Cawood Ledford said during the broadcast. "They have sat through 40 minutes of regulation play, 4 minutes and 59 seconds of overtime play, and they walk out. This could be the most thrilling play of the season, you know."

CLOSE CALLS FOR WILDCATS

The 1958 Wildcats were one of seven Kentucky teams to win a national championship through 2011. That squad lost more games than any of Kentucky's other champions, though. Kentucky finished the 1958 season at 23–6. Three of those losses came by a single point. Kentucky also won several close games. Six of the Wildcats' 23 wins came by five points or less, including two great wins against Temple. Kentucky finished the season ranked number nine in the Associated Press poll.

John Crigler (32) and Johnny Cox (24) of Kentucky battle for a rebound during the 1958 NCAA Tournament final.

It might have been. The Wildcats threw the ball inbounds to senior guard Vernon Hatton. He had just enough time to catch the ball and shoot it. On the air, Ledford described the play: "This time John Crigler will put the ball in play for Kentucky. Ed Beck is under the basket. One second to go, pass to Hatton, from 35 feet, it's good! How about that! How about it! Vernon Hatton did it! It's tied up. Another overtime coming! Stand by! Stand by!"

The two teams played two more overtimes before Kentucky walked off the floor with an 85–83 win. That was no small victory, as Temple finished the season ranked number five in the country.

"Certainly one of the greatest, most thrilling games ever played in Memorial Coliseum," Ledford said on the air.

The Wildcats actually lost three of their next four games. But, they won a series of nail-biters throughout the season. They also won the Southeastern Conference (SEC) title. That propelled them into the National Collegiate Athletic Association (NCAA) Tournament.

During the tournament, the Wildcats hit their stride. They blew out Miami of Ohio and Notre Dame to get into the Final Four. Then they won another close game against Temple, 61–60. That set up a championship showdown against the University of Seattle. Hatton scored 30 points in the game. Meanwhile, junior forward Johnny Cox had 24 points and 16 rebounds. Kentucky beat Seattle 84–72 for Rupp's fourth—and perhaps most improbable—national championship.

In typical fashion for that team, the Wildcats trailed most of the championship game. They had to battle back from two 11-point deficits to win.

HALTON AND COX LEAD

Although Kentucky did not have a collection of stars in 1958, Vernon Hatton and Johnny Cox had exceptional seasons. Hatton, a senior, averaged a team-best 17.1 points per game and earned All-American honors from a couple of smaller publications. Cox, who was a junior, averaged 14.9 points per game. Both are among the top 50 scorers in school history through 2011. Because of their contributions to a championship team, Hatton (No. 52) and Cox (No. 24) have had their jerseys retired by the school.

Kentucky coach Adolph Rupp and guard Adrian Smith (50) celebrate with fans after the Wildcats won the 1958 NCAA title.

"This will absolutely, beyond a doubt go down as *the* coaching year for Adolph Rupp," Ledford said on the air after the game. "Took a team that many thought was not strong enough to win the conference title, was not strong enough to put a single man on the all-conference team, but has been strong enough to come out and take the national championship for the fourth time."

Kentucky has a long winning tradition that includes more than 50 All-American players. However, outside of Hatton and Cox, the 1958 Wildcats were not loaded with talent. Yet, they refused to lose, and because of that, they hold a special place in Kentucky's rich history.

"That, of course, shows that a bunch of boys, even if they aren't brilliant, they still can win if they're determined to win," Rupp said.

Legendary Kentucky coach Adolph Rupp was known as "the man in the brown suit."

2

THE MAN IN THE BROWN SUIT

ADOLPH RUPP ONCE SAID, "DEFEAT AND FAILURE TO ME ARE ENEMIES."

Even before Rupp began his coaching career at Kentucky, his winning attitude was evident. He did not tolerate losing. And he did not tolerate losing outfits. He was coaching at Freeport High School in Illinois during the 1920s when he discovered a winning outfit.

"When I was coaching in high school, in those days of course, if you had two suits, you were very fortunate," he said. "The salaries were not too good and clothes were not too plentiful. I wanted to look real nice in my second year of coaching, so I went out and bought a blue suit. We went to that game and we were shellacked, so I said, 'Uh oh, this blue isn't the kind of suit to wear at a basketball game.' So, I went back to brown and I've been wearing brown ever since, and goodness knows I've got a lot of brown suits in my closet."

WILDCATS GET STARTED

Basketball has been a big part of the culture at the University of Kentucky since 1903, when the game was first introduced to the school then known as State College. On February 6, 1903, Kentucky lost to Georgetown College, 15–6, in its first game. Several men took turns coaching the team from 1903 to 1930. Through those years, the Wildcats had some very good seasons—they went 9–0 in 1912, 12–2 in 1914, 9–2–1 in 1918, and 13–1 in 1921. From 1927 to 1930, John Mauer led the Wildcats to a 40–14 record. He then turned the program over to a young coach, Adolph Rupp. During the early years, three of the best Wildcats were Basil Hayden, Burgess Carey, and Carey Spicer. Hayden was the first All-American at Kentucky.

Rupp became the head coach at Kentucky in 1930. He spent 42 years with the Wildcats and led them to 876 wins. And he wore brown suits during his entire time with the team. He became known as "the man in the brown suit."

Wearing brown was not the only thing that led to Rupp's success. He had great players and built a great tradition. "We here at the University of Kentucky are fortunate," Rupp said. "We have a great basketball tradition. Almost every boy in this area lives for the day when he can come to the University of Kentucky and represent it on the hardwood."

To win nearly 900 games, Rupp also had to demand a lot from his teams. His expectations, nearly every year, were very high.

"We do not wish merely to participate in sports," Rupp said. "We wish to be successful in sports! In order to be successful we must create within these boys the competitive spirit that will bring success. . . . Without victory, basketball has little meaning."

Kentucky's basketball team had achieved some success before Rupp. The Wildcats' first season was in 1902–03. During the 28 seasons before Rupp was hired, Kentucky had a winning record 15 times. That included an undefeated 9–0 season in 1911–12.

Coach John Mauer had led the Wildcats to three winning seasons from 1927–28 to 1929–30, but he quit after that. Rupp was invited to apply for the job. He beat out dozens of other applicants.

With Rupp as head coach, Kentucky never had a losing season. The team's worst season came in 1967, when the Wildcats won 13 games and lost 13 games.

Rupp's first game was on December 18, 1930. He led Kentucky to a 68–19 win over Georgetown College from Kentucky. "I was scared to death," Rupp said years later. "I came down here and I didn't know a thing about any of these teams that we were playing."

He quickly learned, and Kentucky won 15 of its 18 games that first season. There was no NCAA Tournament at the time. But the Wildcats were one of the best teams in the country. Kentucky joined

RUPP'S BEGINNINGS

Adolph Rupp grew up in Kansas and graduated from the University of Kansas. Like Kentucky, Kansas has a strong basketball tradition. At Kansas, Rupp learned the game from Dr. James Naismith, who invented basketball before becoming Kansas' coach, and legendary Kansas coach Phog Allen. At Kentucky, Rupp developed the fast break, which he used to make the Wildcats a winning program.

the SEC for the 1932–33 season and won the conference tournament that season. From 1933 to 1952, the Wildcats won 13 SEC Tournament championships. The SEC did not have a tournament between 1953 and 1978.

Kentucky began getting noticed on a national level during the 1940s. The NCAA Tournament was first played in 1939. At the time, just eight teams were invited. Kentucky received its first invitation in 1942.

Rupp led the Wildcats to their first national championship in 1948. Junior guard Ralph Beard and Alex Groza, a junior center, were named All-Americans. Led by that duo, Kentucky stormed to the title. In the championship game, the Wildcats knocked out Baylor 58–42. Beard and Groza combined for 26 points.

That 1948 team was hardly a two-man show. In fact, the starting five—Beard, Groza, junior guard/forward Cliff Barker, junior forward/center Wallace "Wah Wah" Jones, and senior guard Kenny Rollins—were called the "Fabulous Five." Many consider that team one of the best collections of talent in Kentucky history.

Shortly after beating Baylor, Kentucky's Fabulous Five was selected for the US Olympic team. Professional players could not play for the Olympic team at the time. Rupp was one of the coaches for the US team. Led by Rupp and Kentucky's top players, the United States won the gold medal that year in London, England. The team went 8–0.

With four of the Fabulous Five back in 1949, Kentucky rolled to the NCAA title once again. Groza scored 25 points in the championship

Kentucky's All-American guard Ralph Beard drives under the basket for a layup during a 1947 game.

game, and the Wildcats defeated Oklahoma A&M (now known as Oklahoma State University) 46–36.

The Fabulous Five were gone by 1950. Yet Kentucky might have been the best team in the country that year too. However, the Wildcats never got a chance to prove it at the NCAA Tournament. Kentucky had a 25–5 record and won the SEC championship. But the Wildcats were not invited to the NCAA Tournament. At the time, the NCAA Tournament still only included eight teams.

"When you've won two consecutive NCAA titles and then aren't invited back to defend that championship, there's something wrong with the committee," Rupp said years later. "I have no hesitancy in saying at all that we would have won in '50."

Kentucky's season ended in the National Invitation Tournament (NIT). The City College of New York beat the Wildcats 89–50 in the quarterfinals. It was the worst loss in Rupp's 42 years at Kentucky.

The Wildcats did not have any trouble recovering from that loss. They went 32–2 during the next season, won the SEC again, and captured a third national championship. All-American Bill Spivey, a 7-foot junior center, guided Kentucky to that title. He scored 22 points in the championship game, a 68–58 win over Kansas State.

Kentucky had just six healthy players during the championship game. It showed early, as Kansas State jumped to a 20–12 lead. Kentucky freshman Cliff Hagan was battling an infected throat, but the Wildcats needed him. So, Rupp put Hagan into the game, and Hagan scored 10 points to help the Wildcats win.

All but one player from the 1951 squad returned the next season. With so many players back, the Wildcats had their eyes on another

VOICE OF THE WILDCATS

To many Kentucky basketball fans, Cawood Ledford is as famous as anyone who ever put on a Wildcat uniform. Ledford became the Wildcats' radio broadcaster in 1953. He was the voice of the Wildcats for 40 seasons, through 1991–92. His final game for the Wildcats was a famous 1992 loss to Duke in the NCAA Tournament. Duke hit a jumper with no time left to win in overtime, 104–103.

Center Cliff Hagan starred at Kentucky from 1950 to 1954. He was later enshrined in the Basketball Hall of Fame.

NCAA title. But that was not to be. Spivey sat out the first part of the 1951–52 season after having knee surgery. He missed the rest of the season after he got caught up in a gambling scandal. It was never proven that Spivey helped fix games to help gamblers, but he was suspended anyway. The school reviewed Spivey's case just before the NCAA Tournament. Still, it decided to keep him suspended.

The Wildcats remained one of the best teams, even without Spivey. But their national title dreams were shattered. In the second round of the NCAA Tournament, St. John's upset Kentucky 64–57.

Kentucky was dealt a huge defeat before the next season. During the early 1950s, several college basketball players and teams were found guilty of fixing games to help gamblers. Kentucky got caught up in that too. Spivey was never found guilty, but three other former Wildcats were. As punishment, Kentucky was forced to cancel its 1952–53 basketball schedule.

That was supposed to be the final season for Wildcats stars Frank Ramsey and Hagan. But the two stars from the 1951 championship team did not want to be limited to just practicing during their last year at Kentucky. So both of them dropped their classes for the year. That way they could come back and play the next year.

Kentucky recovered quickly from the scandal. Hagan, a senior center, scored 24 points per game. Ramsey, a senior guard, scored 19.6 points per game. Led by that duo, Kentucky went 25–0 in 1953–54. The Wildcats capped the season with a playoff win over Louisiana State for the SEC title. That win earned Kentucky a trip to the NCAA Tournament. However, the Wildcats declined the invitation. An NCAA rule at the time would have forced Kentucky to play in the tournament without three players because they graduated before it began.

Four years later, Kentucky won its fourth—and final—national title under Rupp's guidance. Vernon Hatton and his teammates put Kentucky back on top in 1958.

Although the Wildcats never won another championship with Rupp, they produced several more great seasons. All-Americans Louie Dampier, a junior guard, and Pat Riley, a junior forward, led the 1965–66 Wildcats to a 27–2 record. They got back to the national championship game that year but lost to Texas Western College (known today as the

Adolph Rupp waves to the crowd before coaching the Kentucky Wildcats for the final time in 1972.

University of Texas at El Paso), 72–65. Texas Western became the first team to win an NCAA title with five black starters.

Six years later, Rupp finished his run at Kentucky. He coached the Wildcats for 41 seasons, from 1930 to 1972. He might have kept coaching the Wildcats, but he was forced to retire. He reached the school's mandatory retirement age of 70 and was not allowed to continue.

Rupp left Kentucky with 876 wins. That record stood until North Carolina coach Dean Smith broke it in 1997. Rupp led Kentucky to 27 SEC titles and coached 23 All-American players.

"We had a lot of fun," Rupp said. "To those of you that went down the glory road with me, my eternal thanks. Goodnight."

Joe B. Hall replaced Adolph Rupp as Kentucky's coach in 1972. He led the Wildcats to 297 wins.

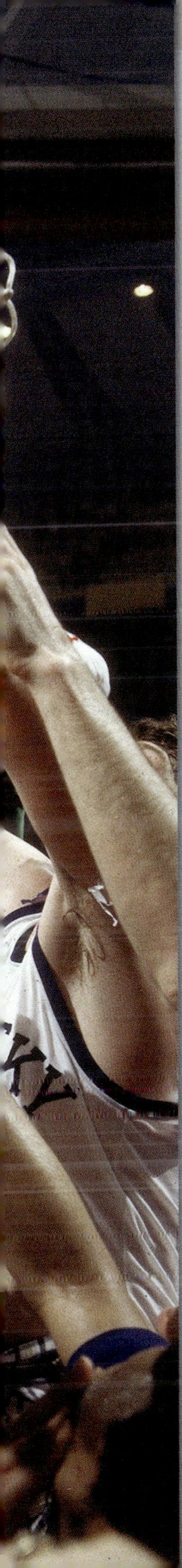

3

HALL GUIDES 'CATS

REPLACING A LEGEND IS NEVER EASY. BUT THAT WAS THE TASK AHEAD OF JOE B. HALL IN 1972. AFTER 41 SUCCESSFUL SEASONS UNDER COACH ADOLPH RUPP, KENTUCKY TURNED TO HALL TO LEAD ITS MEN'S BASKETBALL TEAM.

Hall was a natural fit for the job. He was born in Cynthiana, Kentucky, which is approximately 30 miles (48.3 km) from Lexington. He later played briefly for the Wildcats. In his only varsity season, Kentucky won the 1949 national championship. Hall was then an assistant for Rupp from 1965 to 1972 before taking over the head job.

Hall was also very different from Rupp. And, despite Rupp's success, some players were ready for a change. "Coach Rupp was just getting old," one player said. "He's a great man, but I would say that the players believe Coach Hall will be able to take us further than Coach Rupp could have."

BIG BLUE MADNESS

Coach Joe B. Hall left a lasting impression on Kentucky basketball. He retired after the 1985 season, but every year the Wildcats and their fans enjoy an event started by Hall. Before the 1982–83 season, Hall held a practice at midnight on the first day teams around the country were allowed to practice. He invited fans to attend, and more than 8,500 would show up. At the time, it was called "Midnight Special." It has since become known as "Big Blue Madness," and it has become one of the most anticipated events of the year. More than 23,000 fans attend the event annually, and tickets are gobbled up in a matter of hours. Thousands more watch it on television around the region.

Another player, Ronnie Lyons, said, "Coach Hall is kind of down to our level of thinking more than Coach Rupp. You can relate more to him than you could to Coach Rupp."

For Hall, it was a style that worked. "I was a head coach at small colleges before I came to Kentucky and I learned then to be everything to my players," he said. "I've been a trainer. I've been a tutor. I've been a doctor. I've got a background of closeness to the players and I don't think I'll ever lose that."

If Rupp and Hall were similar in any way, it was that they were winners. Hall coached the Wildcats for 13 seasons, and he won nearly 75 percent of his games (297 wins, 100 losses). Hall guided the Wildcats to the NCAA Tournament 10 times and the Final Four three times. In 1978, he led them to their fifth national championship.

Like Rupp, Hall never had a losing season at Kentucky. And like Rupp, he provided Wildcat fans with some lasting memories.

Kentucky's annual Big Blue Madness event at Rupp Arena features a popular slam dunk contest.

One of those came on March 22, 1975, in the NCAA Tournament's Elite Eight. Kentucky ran into the top-ranked Indiana Hoosiers. The Hoosiers were 31–0 that season. In all, they had won 34 straight games. On this afternoon, however, Kentucky was king. Senior guard Mike Flynn scored a team-high 22 points. Meanwhile, All-American Kevin Grevey, a senior forward, had 17 points to help Kentucky pull off the 92–90 upset.

"Indiana played a good basketball game, but we played a great basketball game," Hall said.

Indiana won the national title the next season with a 32–0 record. In fact, during a stretch of 68 games over the course of four seasons,

Indiana went 67–1. The Hoosiers' only loss was the one against Kentucky.

A week after beating Indiana, Kentucky crushed Syracuse in the Final Four. The Wildcats' magic ran out on March 31, however. Although Grevey scored 34 points, the Wildcats lost to the University of California, Los Angeles (UCLA) 92–85 in the national championship game. It was the last game for legendary UCLA coach John Wooden.

Forward Jack Givens and center/forward Rick Robey were freshmen on the 1974–75 squad. As sophomores, Givens and Robey helped the Wildcats win the NIT. Next to the NCAA Tournament, the NIT was the biggest tournament of the year. Then, in 1977, they led Kentucky to the Elite Eight of the NCAA Tournament.

"Our class has done everything except put that big candle in the middle of the cake," Robey said before his senior season in 1977–78. "As freshmen we were NCAA runners-up to UCLA, as sophomores we won the NIT, and last season we were ranked as high as number two. There's only one thing left to do."

ALL-AMERICANS

Kentucky produced seven All-American players during Hall's 13 years. Three of them—Jack Givens, Kyle Macy, and Rick Robey—played on the Wildcats' 1978 NCAA championship team. Sam Bowie, Kevin Grevey, Melvin Turpin, and Kenny Walker also earned All-American honors during those years. Through 2011, Walker is the second-leading scorer in school history (2,080 points), while Givens is third (2,038).

The Wildcats' Rick Robey dunks over a Duke player during the 1978 NCAA Tournament final.

Robey and Givens indeed capped off their careers with a national title. Both earned All-American honors in leading the Wildcats to a 30–2 record and the national championship. Sophomore guard Kyle Macy earned All-American honors that season too. Kentucky defeated its opponents by an average of 14.3 points per game throughout the season.

Kentucky forward Jack Givens shoots against Duke during the 1978 NCAA Tournament championship.

In the championship game, Kentucky defeated Duke 94–88. Givens was brilliant in the victory, scoring a career-high 41 points. Robey added 20 points. That was nearly six points better than his season average of 14.4.

"Jack Givens played the best game I have ever seen anyone play," said Jim Spanarkel, a junior on Duke's team. "I guess we played him on a night we shouldn't have played him." After the championship game, Givens said, "We won it for the people of Kentucky."

For a school that prides itself on its basketball tradition, the championship was much needed. It had been 20 years since the last one. "We are expected to win, but I wouldn't want to be at a school that didn't care," Hall said.

Hall coached the Wildcats for seven more seasons. He led them to the NCAA Tournament six more times, including another Final Four appearance in 1984. By the time Hall retired at the end of the 1985 season, he had compiled a highly successful 13-year run. He was expected to win, and he did. Hall kept the winning tradition at Kentucky alive and well.

RIVALRY RENEWED

Lexington, the home of the Kentucky Wildcats, and Louisville, home to the University of Louisville, are located less than 80 miles (128.7 km) apart. However, Kentucky refused to put Louisville on the schedule for years. After playing each other twice in 1922, the teams met just three times over the next 60 years. Two games were in the NCAA Tournament—in 1951 and 1959. Their 1948 contest was part of the US Olympic Trials. In 1983, the two schools were pitted against each other in the NCAA Tournament for the first time in 24 years. Then, in 1983, the Wildcats and Cardinals played each other in a regular-season game. They have played each other every year since.

Kentucky guard Rex Chapman battles with Vanderbilt's Barry Goheen over a loose ball during a 1988 game.

4

PITINO'S BOYS

KENTUCKY HIRED EDDIE SUTTON IN 1985 TO REPLACE JOE B. HALL. SUTTON HAD TURNED THE ARKANSAS RAZORBACKS INTO CONSISTENT WINNERS. HE INITIALLY KEPT KENTUCKY ON THE WINNING TRACK TOO. IN HIS FIRST SEASON, 1985–86, SUTTON LED THE WILDCATS TO A 32–4 RECORD AND A TRIP TO THE SWEET 16. OVERALL, SUTTON'S FOUR YEARS WERE A SUCCESS. HE WON 88 GAMES AND LOST JUST 39.

Sutton's time at Kentucky came to a disastrous end, however. Before the 1988–89 season, there were rumors of Kentucky breaking NCAA rules. While the NCAA investigated, the Wildcats struggled. They finished the season with 13 wins and 19 losses. It was their first losing season since 1926–27.

Sutton resigned after the season. Soon after, the NCAA determined that Kentucky broke several rules, such as making illegal payments to recruits. So the NCAA banned the Wildcats from postseason play for two years.

Kentucky's troubles did not scare away Rick Pitino. He was head coach with the New York Knicks of the National Basketball Association (NBA). He had also been a successful college coach before that. Pitino agreed to replace Sutton as Kentucky's head coach.

"I think it's going to be a great challenge for all us—seeing something so rich in tradition brought back in a correct manner," Pitino said on the day he was hired. "The sanctions and probation just make it tougher, but we will overcome all obstacles to make Kentucky basketball rich again."

The Wildcats went 14–14 in Pitino's first season. He did not need much time to restore the glory to the Wildcats. They went 22–6 in Pitino's second season, 1990–91. In his third, Kentucky was eligible for the postseason again.

Led by sophomore forward Jamal Mashburn, Kentucky was one of the best teams in the country in 1992. The Wildcats got all the way to the Elite Eight. Top-ranked Duke needed a remarkable shot at the buzzer in overtime to beat the Wildcats 104–103.

LOCAL HERO

In 1986, Rex Chapman was considered the best high school basketball player in Kentucky. He was also considered one of the best players in the country. A 6-foot-5 guard from Owensboro, Kentucky, Chapman decided to play in college for the Wildcats. Chapman lived up to his potential at Kentucky too. He earned first-team all-conference honors twice and received All-American honors as a sophomore. Chapman left Kentucky after his sophomore year to play in the NBA, where he played 12 productive seasons.

Kentucky's John Pelphrey hugs coach Rick Pitino as Jamal Mashburn (24) looks on after winning the 1992 SEC Tournament.

Losing to Duke was a crushing defeat. But it signaled that Kentucky was back among the nation's elite. During Pitino's eight seasons with the Wildcats, he led them to great success. Kentucky went to the NCAA Tournament six times and to the Final Four three times under Pitino.

Going into the 1995–96 season, Kentucky had not won an NCAA championship for 18 years. Still, many people believed Kentucky had the best team in the country that year. The Wildcats were ranked number one in the country before the season began.

"I tried to use pressure as a motivator for our staff and players," Pitino said after the season. "Every fan they see on campus says, 'Win it all. Win it all.' I wanted the pressure to be a vehicle."

MONSTER MASH

Few players in Kentucky history have been as good as Jamal Mashburn. Born in New York, Mashburn signed with the Wildcats in 1990. At the time, Kentucky was still facing penalties from the NCAA. Mashburn signed anyway. As a freshman, Mashburn scored 12.9 points per game. He only got better from there, scoring 21.3 per game as a sophomore and 21.0 as a junior.

Mashburn was the key player in Kentucky's return to dominance during the 1991–92 and 1992–93 seasons. After his junior season in 1993, Mashburn left school to join the NBA, where he had a stellar 11-year career. He had his No. 24 jersey retired by the Wildcats.

That is exactly what happened. Kentucky lost just two games that season, finishing with a record of 34–2. That included a 16–0 mark in SEC play. The Wildcats were the first team in 40 years to finish the conference schedule undefeated. They also set a school record with 27 consecutive wins during the same season.

Kentucky rolled through their first four games of the NCAA Tournament. They won all those games by at least 20 points. In the championship game, Kentucky outlasted Syracuse, 76–67. Kentucky senior guard Tony Delk drained seven three-pointers and scored 24 points in the win. It was Kentucky's sixth national championship.

Five players from Kentucky's 1995–96 squad went on to play at least eight seasons in the NBA. They were Delk, junior guard/forward Derek Anderson, senior forward Walter McCarty, freshman forward Ron Mercer, and sophomore forward Antoine Walker. Four others on that team spent time in the NBA as well. But Delk was the true star of that team. He scored 17.8 points per game

Wildcats guard Tony Delk goes above the Syracuse defense for a basket during the 1996 NCAA championship game.

that season to lead the way. Delk was also a great defender who finished his career with a school-record 201 steals. He was an All-American that season, and he was also named the SEC Player of the Year.

Kentucky nearly won another national championship in 1997. With Mercer and Anderson leading the team, the Wildcats went 35–5 and advanced to the NCAA championship game. But Arizona knocked off Kentucky 84–79 in overtime.

Pitino left Kentucky shortly after that loss to Arizona. He accepted a rich offer to coach the Boston Celtics in the NBA. Pitino spent just eight seasons in Lexington, but he delivered on his promise to make Kentucky basketball rich again.

Kentucky's Nazr Mohammed dunks during the 1998 national semifinal against Stanford.

5

TUBBY TO CAL

BY THE TIME RICK PITINO LEFT KENTUCKY IN 1997, THE WILDCATS WERE ONE OF THE BEST TEAMS IN THE COUNTRY. THEY WERE NATIONAL CHAMPIONS IN 1996. THEY WERE NATIONAL RUNNERS-UP IN 1997.

With Pitino leaving, however, there was concern about the future of the program. To replace Pitino, Kentucky turned to Tubby Smith. He had been an assistant at Kentucky during Pitino's first two seasons. After those years, Smith had success as the head coach at Tulsa University and at the University of Georgia.

The job at Kentucky came with pressure though. Smith was expected to win a lot and win immediately. "I hope we can reach those expectations," Smith said when he was hired. "Coach Pitino set the bar pretty high. I'll challenge [the players] to raise the bar another level and work even harder than they have in the past."

Kentucky did raise the bar in its first year with Smith. Few people expected the Wildcats to reach the NCAA championship game for a third straight season in 1998. But they did. The Wildcats barely got past Duke and Stanford to reach the final in Smith's first season in charge.

In the final, junior forward Scott Padgett and senior guard Jeff Sheppard led Kentucky to a 78–69 win over Utah. Kentucky overcame a 10-point deficit to win. It was fitting that the Wildcats had to come back. Kentucky trailed in the Sweet 16 against Duke. The Wildcats also trailed in the Final Four against Stanford. In both games, as well as the final game against Utah, the Wildcats had to rally to win.

"We always played poised and knew never to give up," junior forward Heshimu Evans said. "We just come back. We're a fighting team. We're the Comeback 'Cats."

Smith's first year as Kentucky's coach was his best. Like Adolph Rupp, Joe B. Hall, and Pitino, he guided the Wildcats to the NCAA championship.

MAKING HISTORY

Tubby Smith made history before he ever coached a game at Kentucky. In 1997, he became the first African American to be hired as head coach of the Kentucky men's basketball team. Smith said it was "quite an honor." But, he also did not want that to be the focus of his time at Kentucky. "It's more important that I be judged on my character than the color of my skin," he said. Smith fit right in with the Wildcats. He led them to 263 wins and just 83 losses in 10 seasons.

Wildcats players carry coach Tubby Smith off the court after Kentucky won the 1998 NCAA title.

"This program is more than a basketball program," Smith said after the 1998 championship game. "It is really a way of life, and people live and breathe Kentucky basketball. I'm just happy to be a small part of it."

Smith was a big part of the tradition, and he coached the Wildcats for nine more seasons. For most schools, Smith's 10-year run would be considered a huge success. The Wildcats reached the NCAA Tournament in each of Smith's 10 seasons. They advanced to the Sweet 16 six times.

But Smith soon found out that the expectations at Kentucky are sky-high. After winning the national title, Smith failed to get the Wildcats to the Final Four in each of his last nine seasons. In 2005–06, the Wildcats lost 13 games. They lost 12 games in 2006–07. Those seasons were considered disappointments for many Wildcat fans. So, after the 2006–07 season, Smith left. He resigned at Kentucky and became the head coach at Minnesota.

Smith did not win as much as Kentucky fans wanted. But when he left, the Wildcats had been to the NCAA Tournament 16 years in a row. In looking for Smith's replacement, Kentucky hoped to find a coach who would continue that streak. The Wildcats hired Billy Gillispie. He had turned around the programs at the University of Texas at El Paso and Texas A&M.

"You want to be at a place that expects to win every single game," Gillispie said when he was hired. "You want to be at a place that gives you the opportunity to win every single game, and this is the place."

TUBBY'S ALL-AMERICANS

Three players gained All-American status during coach Tubby Smith's time at Kentucky. Forward Scott Padgett was a key player on the 1998 championship team. Forward Tayshaun Prince arrived in 1998–99, but he helped the Wildcats to four NCAA Tournament appearances. He scored 1,775 career points, ranking eighth in school history through 2011. Guard Keith Bogans also helped the Wildcats reach the NCAA Tournament four years in a row. He scored 1,923 career points—fourth most in school history.

Kentucky forward Tayshaun Prince drives to the basket during a 2002 game against Vanderbilt.

Gillispie might have liked the expectations, but Kentucky did not live up to them. In two years, Gillispie went 40–27 and failed to reach the NCAA Tournament in 2008–09. That broke a streak of 17 straight years in the tournament. Kentucky fired Gillispie after that season.

Kentucky hired John Calipari to replace him. Calipari had spent nine years at Memphis, leading the Tigers to nine winning seasons. He guided the Tigers to the 2008 NCAA championship game too. Calipari said he could not pass up the chance to coach at Kentucky, especially after talking to several former Wildcats coaches.

"I talked to coach [Joe B.] Hall. I talked to Tubby Smith. I talked to Eddie Sutton," Calipari said. "And I talked to Rick Pitino about this job. And . . . none of those coaches would trade their time here for anything in the world."

Calipari quickly turned things around in Lexington. During his first year, 2009–10, Calipari guided the Wildcats to a 35–3 record and to the Elite Eight. The Wildcats featured two All-Americans that season. They were freshman point guard John Wall and freshman center DeMarcus Cousins. Both players left after that season for the NBA.

Many wondered how Kentucky would fare in 2010–11 without Cousins and Wall. The Wildcats lost a few more games and finished 29–9. But they got on a roll once the NCAA Tournament began. Behind freshman guard Brandon Knight and freshman forward Terrence Jones, the Wildcats reached the Final Four for the first time since 1998.

The eventual champion Connecticut Huskies edged Kentucky 56–55 in the Final Four. But Calipari and Kentucky had shown that they were again a force on the national stage.

RECORD BREAKER

On January 13, 2009, junior guard Jodie Meeks set a Kentucky school record with 54 points against Tennessee. That broke Dan Issel's single-game record of 53. Meeks also set a school record with 10 three-pointers in the game. That season, Meeks earned All-American honors.

Freshman point guard John Wall led Kentucky to the Elite Eight in 2010. It was his only season in Lexington.

The fact that they reached the Final Four one year after losing Cousins and Wall was even more reason for fans to be optimistic. The winning tradition that began during the 1920s appeared alive and well.

TIMELINE

1903
On February 6, State College (later known as the University of Kentucky) plays its first game of basketball, losing to Georgetown College.

1921
Basil Hayden becomes the first of Kentucky's 49 All-American men's basketball players through 2011.

1930
Kentucky hires Adolph Rupp, a high school coach from Illinois, to coach its basketball team.

1933
Kentucky wins the first SEC Tournament, defeating Mississippi State in the finals.

1942
Kentucky earns its first berth into the NCAA Tournament.

1969
Kentucky earns its 1,000th win—the first team to reach that mark.

1970
Dan Issel finishes his career with 2,138 points, which remained a Kentucky record in 2011.

1972
Forty-two years after he was hired, Rupp coaches his last game for the Wildcats.

1978
Behind Jack Givens's 41 points, Kentucky defeats Duke for its fifth NCAA championship.

1989
Rick Pitino is hired as Kentucky's head coach.

Kentucky wins its first NCAA championship, defeating Baylor in the final.

1948

After an investigation into gambling, the NCAA suspends Kentucky's program for the 1952–53 season.

1952

Vernon Hatton leads the way as Kentucky wins its fourth national championship.

1958

Kentucky is upset in the NCAA championship game by Texas Western College, the first team ever to win a title with five black starters.

1966

Coach Adolph Rupp becomes the winningest coach in college basketball history.

1967

In one of the most famous games in college basketball history, Duke hits a last-second shot in overtime to defeat Kentucky 104–103 in the Elite Eight. It was the last game for longtime Kentucky radio announcer Cawood Ledford.

1992

Kentucky holds off Syracuse to win the NCAA championship for the sixth time.

1996

Coach Tubby Smith, in his first season as Kentucky coach, leads the Wildcats to their seventh national title, defeating Utah in the final.

1998

John Calipari is hired as the Wildcats' coach.

2009

The Wildcats reach the Final Four for the first time since 1998 but lose to Connecticut.

2011

QUICK STATS

PROGRAM INFO

State College (1903–08)
State University Wildcats (1908–16)
University of Kentucky Wildcats (1916–)

NCAA TOURNAMENT FINALS

(WINS IN BOLD)

1948, **1949**, **1951**, **1958,** 1966, 1975, **1978**, **1996**, 1997, **1998**

OTHER ACHIEVEMENTS

Final Fours: 13
NCAA Tournaments: 52
SEC Titles: 44
SEC Tournament titles: 28

KEY PLAYERS

(POSITION(S); YEARS WITH TEAM)

Keith Bogans (G; 1999–2003)
Rex Chapman (G; 1986–88)
Johnny Cox (F; 1956–59)
Tony Delk (G; 1992–96)
Jack Givens (F; 1974–78)
Kevin Grevey (F; 1972–75)
Alex Groza (C; 1944–45, 1946–49)
Cliff Hagan (C; 1950–54)
Dan Issel, (C; 1967–70)
Jamal Mashburn (F; 1990–93)
Ron Mercer (F; 1995–97)
Cotton Nash (C/F; 1961–64)
Tayshaun Prince (G/F; 1998–2002)
Kenny Walker (F; 1982–86)
John Wall (G; 2010)

KEY COACHES

Joe B. Hall (1972–85):
297–100; 21–9 (NCAA Tournament)
Rick Pitino (1989–97):
219–50; 22–5 (NCAA Tournament)
Adolph Rupp (1930–72):
876–190; 30–18 (NCAA Tournament)
Tubby Smith (1997–07):
263–83; 23–9 (NCAA Tournament)

HOME ARENA

Rupp Arena (1976–)

* All statistics through 2010–11 season

QUOTES & ANECDOTES

Whenever the Kentucky basketball team plays on a national stage in a big game, there is a good chance the Wildcats' most famous fan will be there. Actress Ashley Judd, a Kentucky graduate, has been a fixture at Wildcats games for years. She is so well known as a Wildcats fan that she appeared on the college basketball preview edition of *Kentucky Monthly* magazine in November 1998.

In recent years, Kentucky's most heated rival has been in-state foe Louisville. Throughout history, however, the Wildcats have played the Cardinals just 42 times. Kentucky has played Tennessee more than any other team. The Wildcats and the Volunteers have met 212 times, with Kentucky winning 146 of those.

Former Kentucky coach Adolph Rupp made it clear how he feels about the importance of winning. "Why play if it doesn't make any difference? I'm not going to be fooling around with something that doesn't [make] any difference whether you win or whether you lose. I'm not going to be connected with one of those outfits. If it doesn't make any difference, why put scoreboards up there? Why keep score? Why, it makes all the difference in the world."

In addition to wearing a brown suit throughout his 42-year career at Kentucky, Rupp carried a four-leaf clover and a buckeye in his pocket.

GLOSSARY

All-American
A player chosen as one of the best amateurs in the country in a particular activity.

assists
Passes that lead directly to made shots.

conference
In sports, a group of teams that play each other each season.

deficit
The amount by which a team trails another team.

draft
A system used by professional sports leagues to select new players in order to spread incoming talent among all teams. The NBA Draft is held each June.

eligible
Having the right to do something; satisfying the appropriate conditions.

overtime
A period in a basketball game that is played to determine a winner when the four quarters end in a tie.

postseason
The tournaments scheduled after the regular season and conference tournament, including the NCAA Tournament and the NIT.

rebounds
When a player secures the basketball after a missed shot.

recruits
Players being sought after by college teams are known as recruits.

retire
To officially end one's career. If a team retires a jersey number, no future player is allowed to wear it for that team.

rival
An opponent that brings out great emotion in a team, its fans, and its players.

scandal
A disgraceful incident.

varsity
The main team that represents a school.

FOR MORE INFORMATION

FURTHER READING

Clark, Ryan. *Game of My Life. Kentucky Wildcats: Memorable Stories of Wildcat Basketball.* New York: Sports Publishing, 2011.

Rice, Russell. *Kentucky University Basketball Vault.* Atlanta, GA: Whitman Publishing, 2008.

Stricklin, Scott, ed. *Echoes of Kentucky Basketball: The Greatest Stories Ever Told.* Chicago: Triumph Books, 2006.

WEB LINKS

To learn more about the Kentucky Wildcats, visit ABDO Publishing Company online at **www.abdopublishing.com**. Web sites about the Wildcats are featured on our Book Links page. These links are routinely monitored and updated to provide the most current information available.

PLACES TO VISIT

College Basketball Experience
1401 Grand Boulevard
Kansas City, MO 64106
816-949-7500
www.collegebasketballexperience.com

This interactive museum allows visitors to experience various aspects of college basketball. It also includes the National Collegiate Basketball Hall of Fame, which highlights the greatest players, coaches, and moments in the history of college basketball. Several people with ties to Kentucky basketball, including coach Adolph Rupp and former players Cliff Hagan and Dan Issel, are enshrined here.

Rupp Arena
430 W. Vine St.
Lexington, KY 40507
859-233-4567
www.rupparena.com

This is the home arena for the Kentucky men's and women's basketball teams. Tours are not available to the public.

INDEX

ABOUT THE AUTHOR

Brian Howell is a freelance writer based in Denver, Colorado, and has written several books for youth. He has been a sports journalist for more than 18 years, writing about high school, college, and professional athletics, including covering major sporting events such as the US Open golf tournament, the World Series, the Stanley Cup playoffs, and the NBA All-Star Game and playoffs. He has earned several writing awards during his career. He lives with his wife and four children in his native Colorado.